flowers on the moon

BILLY CHAPATA

Andrews McMeel
PUBLISHING®

there is nothing ordinary about you.

there is nothing simplistic about you.

there is nothing mediocre about you.

look at how far your resilience has brought you. look at how your being has protected you along the way. look at how you have managed to get this far through all the mistakes, bad decisions, and wrong routes you've taken. look at where your intuition, or choice to ignore it, has brought you. look at how all the pain and heartache you've suffered have birthed a **new you.**

it is no mistake that you are here. your existence is no coincidence, so that should add more sense to your presence—there is much more ahead of you.

much more light, much more goodness, much more sweetness.

much more laughter, much more happiness, much more love.

much more peace, much more connection, much more **growth.**

you will grow wherever you are planted because you are deserving of all these things and more, and if you ever forget, doubt, or need comfort, may these words aid in your **bloom.**

CONTENTS

enceladus.

dear self,

i choose you, and only you. i'm sorry it took so long.

guiltless.

you don't have to feel guilty for not being someone's version of
perfect anymore. you are allowed to exude authenticity without
compromising your truth.

you don't have to feel guilty for not being accessible anymore.
you are allowed to create distance from the ones who disrespect
your boundaries and taint your energy without having to explain
yourself.

you don't have to feel guilty for failing to do what you promised
yourself you would do anymore. you are allowed to fall over and
over, until you learn how to walk again.

you don't have to feel guilty for being selfish with yourself any-
more. you are allowed to give yourself the love you wish to receive
without anyone confusing your revolution with narcissism.

you don't have to feel guilty for finding happiness anymore. you
are allowed to live in your truth without worrying about the ones
you left behind.

(learning to cut ties is one of the most liberating and beautiful things you can ever learn. you have to remove dead roots so you can plant something that actually has the ability to grow)

cutting ties as **therapy.**

cutting ties to **heal.**

cutting ties for **peace.**

magical mileage.

let the distance you've created between

yourself and the people who hurt you

create the **space** you need to heal.

let the energy between the distance

be a reminder to the ones who took

you for granted that you know your worth.

(you can admire beautiful things from afar)

there are women with flowers planted firmly in their **minds,** and their way of thinking is not an invitation for you to water them. there are women with gold buried deep within their souls, and their outer glow is not an invitation for you to dig it out. there are women who can feed your soul with kindness and whose energy feels like sunlight, but that doesn't mean you have permission to use their **warmth** whenever you please.

a prayer:

a lover with no desire to change you.

a lover who wishes to see you grow through the love you have for yourself.

a lover who doesn't wish to complete you

but only wishes to decorate the wholeness you exhibit already.

you are **worthy** of all of this.

<u>*bona fide spirit.*</u>

nothing is more exhausting than

living in skin that doesn't fit you.

nothing feels heavier on your spirit

than pretending to be something that you're not.

nothing starves you more than giving

energy to false versions of you.

nothing is more beautiful than your **authentic self.**

<u>*broken clocks.*</u>

some wounds need more than time to heal.

they need **introspection, patience,** and **love.**

they need understanding, softness, and honesty.

give them what they need and detach any

expectations from your healing.

<u>*faux.*</u>

i'd rather be **alone** than form convenient

connections disguised as friendships.

my soul steers away from anything

unauthentic and disingenuous.

(love her, but don't try to control her)

clothe her in love,

but leave her mind **naked.**

cognizance.

when i started to feel unworthy,

that's when i realized that

i gave you too much power over me.

when i started to feel unworthy,

that's when i realized that

i gave you too much space to stretch

your opinion over my mind.

when i started to feel unworthy,

that's when i knew that i had to

reclaim myself again.

(i just want you to be the best version of yourself)

i'm not trying to be a distraction.

i'm not trying to complete you.

i'm just trying to serenade the love

you have for yourself already

and watch you **blossom** into

the flower you truly want to be.

(wisdom only time could teach me)

your growth doesn't **entitle** you to a second chance with me. the part of me that cares about you is proud of the strides you've made, but the part of me that cares about myself knows not to indulge in your energy ever again.

somewhere along the line,

she stopped apologizing for refusing to be what you expect
her to be.

somewhere along the line,

she stopped apologizing for shattering the false illusions of her that
you had.

somewhere along the line,

she stopped apologizing for holding on to her truth like gold.

somewhere along the line,

she found herself.

darling,

you don't have to be seen to be worthy. you are still whole without their acknowledgment. you will still breathe without their surveillance. you still exist.

come back.

the worst thing you can do is ignore your own feelings.

betray your vibrations, put your emotions on a shelf.

the worst thing you can do is walk away from yourself

when you are the one thing you need the most.

spiritual devotions.

be so **committed** to your growth that it encourages

the ones around you to grow as well.

be so **committed** to your growth that it scares away

the ones that are tempted to drop you down to their level.

___beautiful losses.___

when i started finding myself,

i started losing a lot of people.

that's when i knew that the people i was losing

were not complementing the **god** within me.

(heartbreak was only a catalyst for her to love harder)

i knew she was powerful when she told me that every time
she lost love,

she found that same love **twice** within herself.

(your journey will scare some people. the steps that you take will intimidate others, and the paths that you take will confuse some. people are afraid of things they can't control, and when they realize that they have no power over you, it scares them. it brings out their biggest fears, it unmasks their deepest insecurities, it reveals their true colors. when you live in your truth and it goes against what other people believe in, you're always going to rub some people the wrong way. they'll have opinions, they'll have ideas, they'll have assumptions, but what they think of you is none of your business)

these days, the steps i take are filled with fewer apologies and more intent.

these days, the steps i take are fueled by my intuition and not your opinion.

my growth is much louder than your **projections.**

i'm not here to be a sponge for your **insecurities.**

darling,

if you have to convince them of your worthiness, they might not be worth holding on to. poison comes in shiny bottles too.

(just because it comes back to you, doesn't mean it's meant to be permanent)

old love doesn't always come back to stay. sometimes old love only comes back as a reminder to show you how much you've grown without them. sometimes old love only comes back as a reminder to show you that your existence does not depend on them **watering** you.

(empathy can be your best friend or your biggest enemy. there will be several situations in life that will bring you to a crossroad. a crossroad between what's good for you and what's good for them. understand that there is absolutely nothing wrong with being selfish and doing what's best for you. some people won't understand your decisions initially, and some may never understand at all, but your peace of mind and happiness are not worth sacrificing for anything or anyone. you've worked too hard on yourself to be affected by people and things that don't understand the energy and time you've put into yourself)

never poke at your wholeness to fill someone else's emptiness.

never let anyone dry up your well of energy by compromising

the hard work you've put into **yourself.**

i hope

you find someone who sees light in you

but loves you enough not to dim you

so they can selfishly illuminate dark corners

that exist within them.

i hope you find someone who is inspired

by the light within you

and is encouraged to find light of their own.

(thank you for helping me unearth myself)

you didn't have the patience to stick around to see what i could become for you, but with hindsight, you leaving allowed me to become what i needed to be for **myself.**

subtle warnings.

be careful of the ones with tight grips.

the ones who are scared to let you go.

the ones who think losing you will remove

the air from their lungs if you never come back.

insecurity does well to disguise itself as love,

but love doesn't fear freedom,

it grows **flowers** from it.

to whom this may concern,

why do you treat yourself so carelessly? you've been settling for a bare minimum kinda love, when your own love is unquantifiable. welcome love that meets you at the level that you're at, and welcome love that embraces the level that you're trying to get to.

to whom this may concern,

one day, you will need to make room for happiness in your life; and on that day, you will realize that you're above all the people who hurt you, took you for granted, and mistreated you. your wounds are not you.

to whom this may concern,

understand that the ones who are only drawn to your exterior are shallow and lazy lovers. there's nothing more intimate than being with someone who sees you. not your vessel, your skin, or your flaws, but someone who sees the god in you.

if i love you,

you will never have to question it.

my love cup overflows.

(the situations may change, but the intention doesn't)

as my relationships with others change,

my relationship with myself evolves too.

at times i can't get enough of myself,

and at other times i need a hiatus from me.

at times i understand myself,

and at other times i find need for rediscovery.

at every phase, **i am my own priority.**

darling,

you've bruised your knees too many times begging them not to leave, while your inner child pleads for you to come back home. let goodbyes serve as the catalyst you need to reintroduce yourself to you.

they deserve space to heal too,

your family, friends, and lovers.

they **deserve time** to explore their wounds

without anyone trying to adopt their pain.

they **deserve room** to breathe without anyone

trying to suffocate their wounds with constant opinions and ideas.

(that gut feeling: never ignore it, never betray it)

intuition **told** me who you were,

before you **showed** me who you were.

<u>**free reins.**</u>

you can bloom wherever you desire to.

you can bloom wherever you need to.

you are not confined to your environment.

you are not handcuffed to your past.

you are not obligated to anyone.

you are **free** to bloom.

softly, wildly, unapologetically.

i hope

you never feel unworthy of all the good things you attract, and if you ever feel unworthy, i hope you take the time to patiently heal the parts of you that cause uncertainty.

reminder:

some things cannot be fixed, not because they must remain broken,
but because they are meant to be replaced with something stronger.
some things should not be fixed, not because they can't be, but
because they are the reminder you need to never break yourself for
anyone ever again.

darling,

aren't you exhausted by love that shows up conditionally? one day, you'll become tired of how inconsistent they are with their love, and on that day, i pray you'll realize that you deserve to love yourself with the same consistency they failed to show you.

(you've outgrown them for a reason)

don't betray your progression by running back

to the same ones you've **outgrown.**

lazy love,

your love was not meant for me. my bones are filled with too much passion to let anyone who isn't as enthusiastic about me as i am about myself to hold me. i've tolerated you for too long, while i became intolerable to myself. i've accepted you for too long, while i became less accepting of myself. what kind of love forces you to choose between you and your lover? what kind of love tells you how much love it has for you, only to show you how little love it truly has? what kind of love asks you to lose love for yourself so you can love someone else more? perhaps i've been too lazy in the way i love myself, and that's why you've deemed it perfectly fine to love me with the bare minimums. to love me enough just to keep me around, instead of loving me with the same love you wish to receive from me. i have learned many things about love, and i have learned many things about myself, but one thing i refuse to learn is how to accept love that is less than what i deserve. lazy love—your love was not meant for me.

(it's ironic)

you keep holding on to bad love

thinking that time and patience will turn it sweet,

not knowing that bad love is only **poisoning** the love you have
for yourself.

(i hope you learn)

if you ever enter my life

with intentions other than decorating the space in my mind

and furnishing the thoughts on my mental,

don't be surprised when i decide never

to open my doors to you again.

i'll **choose peace** before i choose you.

<u>*either.*</u>

i'm an ocean that some lovers were too scared to dive in,

and an ocean that swallowed others whole.

my love will either **illuminate** you or **intimidate** you.

understand,

time is not a measuring tool for connections. don't oversell the strength or importance of a connection because of how long you've known them. sometimes it's the ones you've known for a shorter time that show up, while the familiar faces hide in the shadows.

<u>*bittersweet goodbyes.*</u>

the love was there.

we just spoke love in different languages,

and one day, i hope you find ears that can **understand** your energy.

notes on healing:

wounds need air to breathe, to heal. concealing your wounds with bandages only slows down your healing. confront your wounds, bring them out in the open, ask them why they still hurt, ask them what they require to be soothed—**ask your wounds important questions.**

(never let anyone's pain be the reason why you find inadequacies within yourself)

be careful of the things you tell yourself

when people can't love you correctly,

when they can't celebrate you fully,

when they can't appreciate you unconditionally.

their inadequacies are not a **reflection** of you.

don't let people's **projections** become your truth.

impatient.

i grew tired. you came and went as you pleased, so i finally dug out the strength to change the locks. you rented space in my mind, so i had to evict you permanently. i grew tired of being a **comfort zone** for you.

life keys.

never let anyone's misery sprinkle insignificance on your **happiness.**

(you deserve the liberty to ask for help when you need it, but you also deserve the freedom to rediscover yourself on your own when you need to)

patient love. love that holds your hand when you need to learn how to walk again. love that lets go of your hand and allows you to bloom on your own so you can learn how to love yourself again. **you deserve that.**

(words aren't so sweet when they're empty)

if you dress me in beautiful words,

make sure your actions **complement** the clothing you've
picked out for me.

<u>wound palette.</u>

if they have no idea about the things you've endured,

never let them paint your pain as something **ordinary,**

something **common,** something **unimportant.**

your experiences were not meant to be minimized

to make other people less uncomfortable.

question:

you want them to love you unconditionally,

but how unconditional is your love for yourself?

(sometimes you need to break to realize how strong you are)

i had to break several times to realize that i am not broken.

i had to break several times to realize my wholeness.

i had to break several times to realize that i am not defined by how many times i break.

darling,

if you're going to make a home out of anyone, make sure the person you make a home out of is yourself. don't give anyone the permission to come and go with your happiness as they please. let your joy be dependent on no one else but yourself.

deadly concoctions.

when they dilute your truth,

you don't have to drink the mixture they've made for you—
pour it out.

their sentiments, ideas, and opinions of you,

pour them out to **make room** for the sweetness that exists
within you.

<u>*quiet justice.*</u>

and when they deserve no words,

don't fill the air with nuances that will make your silence less
uncomfortable for them.

let your energy **communicate** in ways that your words won't.

epiphanies.

i had to question your love for me, and that's when i knew that
your love wasn't meant for me.

please take your time with this self-love;

some days will be harder than others, but take your time. some days will require you to take a few steps back, but take your time. some days will encourage you to retreat into solitude, but please take your time with this self-love.

**vacancy.**

people take up space.

situations take up space.

energy takes up space.

if it shrinks your being,

don't allow it to stay for too long.

leave room for more of **you** in your life.

karmic energy.

revenge is cheap therapy.

temporary fulfillment.

learn to leave bad alone without trying to get even.

the **universe** deals with everyone accordingly.

darling,

you have so many questions about their love. but all you have to do is look at their inconsistency to get your answers.

(she still blooms)

she's the flower you plucked all the petals from,

but grew them back using all the **love** you never gave her.

to whom this may concern,

if my growth makes you uncomfortable, i'm glad that it does.
my growth is not meant to make you comfortable. i have had
uncomfortable days shedding old skin and many moments planting
my roots in different spaces. i am allowed to grow and not have to
explain why i outgrew you.

dear miss-understood,

i hope you realize that you're more than your flaws, i hope you
realize that you're more than your scars, i hope you realize that
you're too divine to fit in that jar that they have all of your past
mistakes in, i hope you realize that there is much more to you.
there will be times when they try to minimize you to fit their
shallow opinions, but you don't have to swim in waters that feel
so unfamiliar. you can dive into whatever feels comfortable, so
if you feel like backstroking all the way into my mind, you can.
you can lay all your worries to rest with me, no judgment, just
honesty, vulnerability, and light. no reservations and concerns
about what's wrong and right. for too long you've given yourself to
lovers who marvel in the things you don't do right, in lovers who
don't operate on forgiveness but are fueled by spite. you deserve the
patience, love. you deserve the time, love. to make mistakes and
learn from them. you are a work in progress, and anyone unable
to comprehend that doesn't deserve to read the pages in your soul.
they don't deserve to be a part of the chapters that have all your
moments of goodness. they don't deserve any space in your future.
make it understood.

release.

you will never gain closure from the same doors old lovers
closed on you.

stop knocking on those doors and hoping for a new response.

(you never were)

after feeling lost and broken for so long, here you are, making your way back to yourself, slowly, softly, gently. after feeling lost and broken for so long, here you are, blooming, breathing, healing. **darling, you were never broken to begin with.**

deimos.

(you deserve all the beautiful things you attract. you deserve all the goodness coming to you)

i hope you heal the parts of you that are scared to be happy

because of fear that your happiness will never last.

you are deserving of everything good you attract,

no matter how **short** or **temporary** it may be.

(no one is you, and that is your superpower)

i am not for everyone,

and that is my **magic.**

you cannot take that from me.

(some connections never die)

honor the friendships that allow you to pick up from where you last left off, regardless of how long it's been since you connected. the friendships that survive hiatuses, silences, and space. those are the connections that **never die.**

to my future son:

strip the idea that softness and masculinity are mutually exclusive.

revised scripts.

these times don't define you. these nights or days, when you break down and feel like you've lost everything. when you feel hopeless. when you feel weak. you can start over from where you are, without attaching the **past** to your narrative.

(you don't have to stay for something forcing you to leave)

true love doesn't have expiration dates,

but true love also knows when to **let go.**

<u>not for sale.</u>

my potential is not up for grabs.

love me in my current state,

or redirect your energy elsewhere.

(patience, love, patience. love will find you when the time is right)

when loneliness is your catalyst for forming connections, the loneliness never really disappears. it sits there, hidden, covered, camouflaged, until time opens that emptiness wide open again. there is no harm in waiting for the connections that are right for you.

(strange paradoxes)

it's the ones who view your self-love as a threat

who are actually a threat to your self-love.

—ironic.

inner flame.

oh, but darling,

this fire you have in your soul is beautiful.

it was not meant to be extinguished for people who can't handle
your passion.

<u>*priorities.*</u>

i am not attached to the person i am,

nor am i attached to the person i was.

i am only attached to the thought of **evolving** into the fullest
version of myself.

reminder:

never let sentiment disrupt your growth.

your journey forward is more important than the things you've
left behind.

(you are magic, and don't you ever forget it)

you've always felt like you've never belonged, but maybe that's just a **reminder** from the universe that you belong to yourself before you belong to anyone else.

dear self,

it's me again. it's been awhile, hasn't it? i guess my attention has been elsewhere lately. somewhere in the clouds, somewhere in the mountains, somewhere in the seas—everywhere but with you. i know i've been distant, nonexistent, a ghost. i know i've left you cold, alone, neglected. i guess my energy has been misplaced. focusing on others, when you deserve as much attention as i give them. warming up to others, when you deserve as much love as i give them. it's so easy to ask if everyone else is doing good but so hard to approach yourself with the same question, and maybe that's why i've held off on talking to you for so long. perhaps the deeper i look in, the more i'll realize that i've forgotten about you. that all this time, i've been using people as distractions to avoid tending to you. that all this time, the guilt of abandoning you manifested in the way i behaved. i ignored the signs but played to the tune of insecurity. turning the volume louder and louder until i couldn't hear you anymore. but here i am, vulnerable, optimistic, honest, telling you that i apologize for forgetting about you and that i'm ready to love you again.

when do you let go?

when it feels heavy on your soul. when you feel more trapped
than emancipated. when it tastes less sweet and more like poison.
when you feel yourself sinking instead of floating. when freedom
becomes a battle. open your heart to intuition; you'll always know.

when do you hold on?

when hope exists. when it fills your lungs with air, no matter how
deep the struggle is. when joy overweighs sadness. when flowers
grow from hard spaces in your heart. if you don't feel friction, it's
worth holding on to. if it flows, it's worth swimming in.

lately,

you've been swimming beneath the waves to avoid everyone's energy, but i want you to know that drowning your being for anyone won't make you feel more alive.

notes on healing:

healing requires you to spend some time with yourself. alone time with all of your wounds. peeling the bandages off and exposing your wounds to the elements. giving them air to breathe within the confines of your pain. this is your process, your battle, your struggle. no one will ever understand it as much as you do, and no one needs to. there is beauty in that. beauty in the fact that you hold the key to your own healing. beauty in the fact that you have the power to shift your energy in a way that strengthens your resolve. immerse yourself fully in the experience. no one can heal you the way you can heal you.

lost & found.

i am learning to hold myself again.

through the rain,

and through the sun.

through the rough,

and through the softness.

i am learning to hold myself

as **tightly** as i held others.

(just maybe)

maybe it's not about finding the right person but about the right person finding you. maybe it's not about searching for the one but about waiting for someone. someone who complements you, someone who feeds your spirit, someone who gives you a new lease on life and manages to revive parts in your soul that have been dormant for so long. maybe it's about releasing the idea of wanting to be in control and **letting the universe work its magic.**

(i love you, but i love myself more)

i have no desire to save you.

i only wish to show you the light that exists within you,

so you can save **yourself.**

the most beautiful women i've met

had minds like libraries and books in their souls. the kind of women with pages within them that must be flipped slowly and read delicately to discover the magic that exists in their bones.

musing.

you will never have much control of how people treat you,

but you will always have control of how you treat yourself.

be kind to yourself. gentle with yourself. soft to yourself

—be the love that you deserve.

(*you can move to where there is more life*)

and when their energy becomes overwhelming, breathe elsewhere. rest your lungs in spaces that ease you. in spaces full of air and sweetness. in spaces that allow you to inhale love and exhale anything that isn't. do not allow anyone's presence to **suffocate** your own.

lessons my mother taught me:

you cannot grow if you insist on them holding your **roots** for you.

<u>**happy memorials.**</u>

i no longer **grieve** the older versions of me that have died,

i now **celebrate** newer versions of me that those deaths
have birthed.

you'll know it's meant to be

when their love for you encourages you to love yourself even more. when their love for you amplifies the love you have for yourself already. when they're not subtracting from your being but adding on to the beautiful pieces existing within you.

reality check.

i didn't just gain the strength to say goodbye overnight.

my revolution didn't just happen recently,

i was gone long before i left you.

darling,

there is a silver lining in everything you lose. let what needs to leave, leave, let what needs to go, go, and be patient as the universe reveals the blessings you made space for.

(i deserve to be appreciated always, all ways)

i no longer find comfort in places that only celebrate me when it's **convenient.**

**gifts.**

you've spent too much time mourning the ones you've lost

and spent too much energy reminiscing by the tombstones
of old connections

instead of preparing yourself for the **beautiful** ones who are
yet to come.

moonchild,

trust this phase of your life that you're currently in.

no matter how cold or warm this phase feels, embrace it.

give it a hug, listen to it, absorb it, understand it.

you are where you are supposed to be right now.

trust your phases.

(whispers of intuition)

the tighter you hold on, the harder it is to make room for the blessings you actually deserve. release what doesn't want to be kept, and get rid of whatever has overstayed its welcome.

—voicemail left by god

darling,

don't give up on yourself. you're worth all the internal wars you've been fighting lately.

learning:

the art of losing love

but continuing to love yourself.

<u>**regularity.**</u>

how often are you around for yourself?

you're readily available for other people,

but have you tended to you?

have you shown yourself the same amount

of love and compassion that you've shown them?

have you told yourself the same beautiful things

that you've told them?

how often?

(you only have yourself to blame)

i will not apologize for having no space in my heart for you anymore. you pushed yourself out with all of your actions, and i filled all those cold spaces you left with **self-love.**

treasure chests.

many lovers have showed a willingness to explore your body,

while leaving your mind barren and untraveled.

don't let them treat you like a country,

when a whole **world** exists within you.

(she'd rather lose love than lose herself, and that was one of the most beautiful things about her)

i asked her, if not love, what was she afraid of losing the most? she gently replied, **"myself."**

<u>**one too many.**</u>

i have learned too many old lovers' languages, while they hesitated to learn mine. i have learned too many old lovers' energy, while they lacked the patience to learn mine. i have learned too many times that unrequited love is not meant to be romanticized.

see,

they never tell you that sometimes you have to lose love to learn
how to love yourself.

<u>**unions.**</u>

friends who get excited when you talk about your dreams.

friends who applaud your growth even if it means outgrowing
parts of your connection together.

friends who check up on you even when you appear to be happy.

friends like this.

burdensome.

guilt is such a heavy thing to carry.

aren't you tired of taking it with you everywhere you go?

forgive the person you used to be,

so you can become the person you **need** to be.

<u>celebrate.</u>

feel no guilt about the boundaries you've created. instead, **rejoice** in the space you've created for yourself to breathe without having to worry about people's opinions and ideas of you.

spiritual cleanses.

you don't like being lied to,

so why do you feel like your wounds are any different?

your wounds deserve honesty—

feeding yourself the truth and being open with yourself is
how you **heal.**

public service announcement:

it took me several sleepless nights

and several exhausting mornings

to find the courage to step into my truth.

it took me breaking myself apart

and rebuilding myself into something new

to realize my power.

i am past the stage of convincing anyone of my **magic.**

evolve.

you are full of so many chapters. you have been many different poems before. you are a different essence now, a different embodiment; but don't hang on to the poem that you were, because the poem you are becoming will prove to be the most **beautiful** one you've ever written.

(you can't love me the same way you loved old lovers)

i am not a one-size-fits-all kinda lover.

don't one-size-fits-all your love with me.

learn me, feel my nuances, understand my internal language.

i have layers that require **time** and **patience.**

(lessons i've learned)

you taught me that you can't be everything to everyone,

and that's why i'm not trying to be everything to anyone but
myself.

if you're reading this, i'm probably gone by now.

i used to reside in your heart, but i had to move out recently.
between you and me, it became a little too expensive to live there.
it cost me too much happiness, and it cost me so much peace,
and these are things i never budgeted for when you asked me to
move in. the warmth i felt in the air when i first moved in slowly
turned cold, and even though i attempted several times to repair
the broken windows and fix the energy between us, sometimes
situations should be left alone before common ground is found.
we've waited and waited, staring at clocks and hoping time can
replace everything we've lost, but the only thing i've found is that
it's best for me to pack my belongings and go. sleeping in a cold
heart every day and hoping that it will warm up is like playing a
game of russian roulette with my happiness, and i'm not trying to
take any chances. so i moved out and came back to myself, and i
can safely say there's no place like home.

(inner understandings)

do not hold yourself prisoner to the times you've been unable to help the people you care about. do not chain yourself to the guilt of being unable to do more. you cannot help others unless you can help yourself, and the ones who truly love you will always **understand** this.

darling,

you're lonely, and you've been searching for fulfillment in different places, but set your bags down for minute and stop searching. you've been looking for love everywhere but in yourself.

understand,

it is not my duty to make

my truth taste **sweet** for you.

my existence does not hinge

on whether i am your cup of tea or not.

(sometimes we outgrow the people we used to know and become different people. when growth happens, some people take our changes personally. not because they have something against us but because they don't recognize the person we are now. you are not responsible for people's assumptions of you. you are also not obligated to remain the person people remember you to be)

you loved the person i was,

i love the person i'm **becoming.**

individuality.

your path is yours,

and their path is theirs.

comparing the two will always

put roadblocks in the path of your destination.

(breathe)

some apologies never come, some apologies never will. some apologies are buried deep beneath ego and may never be unearthed. some apologies are locked behind pride and don't have spare keys. **breathe,** love. never let the lack of an apology stop you from existing.

gentle reminder:

on the days when you feel sad,

the days when you feel indifferent,

remember that it is not a sin to refuse to smile.

remember that it is not a sin to spend time with yourself to recover.

remember that it is not a sin to feel.

happiness will find a way to hold your hand again.

<u>*finally.*</u>

i am finding my way back to myself again.

slowly, patiently, intricately.

i am finding roads in between my heart and my mind that connect.

i am finding melodies that taste good on my soul.

i stray and i take detours occasionally,

but i am finding my way back to myself again.

(just so you know)

you are mistaken.

i never stopped loving you,

i only stopped entertaining you.

there is a much bigger **difference.**

to the woman at war with her body:

i hope you learn to lay your weapons down, so you may learn that peace exists inward and not by what you see in the reflection. i hope you learn that what you tell yourself will always be more important than what they have to say about you.

self-connection.

when was the last time you were really in love with yourself? i mean really in love with yourself? it's so easy to recollect the last time you were in a connection with someone, the last time you fell head over heels for them, but when was the last time you really fell for yourself? that deep marination between your heart and your soul? that feeling of invincibility and feeling like you can do anything because you're so full of love? when was the last time you felt that? when was the last time you looked within and realized that you were complete without anyone else? that you were whole alone? that you had no pieces missing? when was the last time you were in love with yourself?

bittersweet beginnings.

heartbreak is never the end.

it is only the start of the beautiful relationship

you can finally start with **yourself.**

choices.

do you really move on from the ones you once loved? or does
time just make the void feel less vacant? lovers go, and sometimes
they never return, but whatever happens to the feelings you
had for them? do you just discard them and put them on a shelf
somewhere before you're ready to deal with them? or do you
just put a permanent shell around your heart and decide never
to deal with them again? if the energy and emotions within the
connection were genuine, then, regardless of the circumstances
and the outcome, love should always be constant. love should
always be truth. love should always be the choice. maybe it's not a
case of moving on from those you once loved or time making the
void feel less vacant but making a conscious choice to love yourself
despite those who left, those who never returned, and those
who never loved you the way you deserved. maybe it's a case of
choosing yourself, despite the love you may still have for them.

<u>**bad blood.**</u>

blood isn't immune to boundaries.

you are allowed to **protect** yourself from

family who disrupt your peace intentionally and unintentionally.

freedom.

i have had to let go of much,

to hold on to myself a little **tighter.**

<u>*unapologetic.*</u>

i am not sorry about the parts of me that no longer exist that you
still romanticize.

i am not sorry about the versions of myself that expired that you
still hold on to.

i am only sorry that you haven't grown since the last time you
knew me.

my growth owes you no apologies.

(celebrate yourself often)

clap for yourself so loud that it silences people's opinions.

celebrate yourself so much that it becomes a **habit.**

but you see,

there is magic in finding the balance between never settling and not taking what you already have for granted. you don't have to stay rooted in what no longer serves you, but never forget who or what helped you get to where you are currently.

absorb this:

when your actions are empty,

i will not **water** your words to give them life.

amalthea.

<u>*respire.*</u>

true love never leaves,

sometimes it just gets lost temporarily.

lost in pride and ego,

lost in confusion and misunderstanding.

but love being lost is never the end;

sometimes love needs to **breathe** before it finds home again.

(sometimes we obstruct the growth of the people we love by constantly offering advice, a helping hand, or an opinion. sometimes the best way to help someone bloom is by just letting them be)

allow people to learn their lessons without imposing your energy on them. allow people the room to grow without shrinking their narrative. sometimes love means allowing people the freedom to make their own mistakes so they can become who they need to **be.**

<u>*learning.*</u>

learning to smile through it all.

learning to breathe through it all.

learning to love through it all.

learning.

smoke and mirrors.

illusions shatter so you can finally confront truth. when the things
that you held on to get removed from your grip, take it as a sign.
when the things you believed in for so long get reshuffled
internally, take it as a sign. mirrors must break before
truth is revealed.

reminder:

there are people praying for the same things you take for granted.

darling,

you will never have to change yourself for the right kind
of love. evolve for your own self-preservation, not for anyone
else's standards.

<u>*rescue.*</u>

tell those parts that they couldn't love that you love them.

ask those parts that they couldn't love for forgiveness.

forgiveness for placing your worth in the hands of people

who never had the right to dictate your worth in the first place.

reclaim your power. reclaim your **self.**

(i hope this serves as the confirmation you need)

you've cried oceans for lovers

who would much rather swim to

safety than dive into your pain,

and you should know that you

deserve a love that isn't

uninterested or afraid of all the

waves and vibrations that life presents you.

last year taught me how to swim;

how to float when the water becomes too deep. how to dive when the water becomes too shallow. how to breathe when the rest of the world wants to suffocate you in misery. i learned that happiness comes in waves. i learned that healing comes in waves. i learned that i am both art and a work in progress, and i deserve time to come into my own. i learned that pain is temporary and that happiness is a choice. you can choose to be happy, or you can let your tears create a pool on the floor so deep you can drown and lose yourself in it.

last year taught me to stop running;

away from my fears and closer to reality. away from illusions and directly into truth. i learned that my soul can grow tired too, from trying so hard to avoid situations that seem undesirable, from trying so hard to ignore pending conversations sitting in my soul's inbox, from trying so hard to remain ignorant of the people and things hurting me. i deserve calm and peace of mind.

last year taught me to be honest with myself;

to look at myself inwardly and have conversations that involve vulnerability, sincerity, and truth. to take my wounds out on a date and ask them what's stopping them from healing and why they hurt so bad. to be more empathetic with others and more sympathetic with myself. to acknowledge that i don't have to be perfect, don't have to look perfect, or don't have to seem perfect for anyone. perfection is a poisonous illusion, and softness is one of my greatest superpowers. i don't have to dance with pain even when the music stops playing. i am love, and i need to be more gentle with me.

differences.

love without expectation, but love yourself enough not to tolerate anything unreciprocated for too long. love is not meant to be draining, depleting, or exhausting. love is meant to add on to what already **exists** within you.

affirmation:

what's for me is already mine. nothing and no one can take what rightfully belongs to me.

silent intentions.

when words escape you,

wait for them to find you again.

the right words will come back home when they are ready.

wait for them; don't rush them.

give them time to process what fits right with your soul.

it's okay to keep to yourself until they find you **again.**

<u>*soul knots.*</u>

you are an experience. you deserve to have your mind held
by hands that take their time to unravel all the magic behind
your eyes. you deserve to have your layers peeled back slowly to
understand the language that's closest to home for you. you deserve
to be experienced **fully.**

too long.

for too long you've poured energy outward,

decorating other people while neglecting home.

for too long you've put yourself second

to keep other people smiling.

make room for yourself in your own life.

occupy the spaces you afford to other people once in a while.

prioritize **you.**

(lessons time taught me)

if it's toxic, let it breathe **elsewhere.**

stop waiting for bad love to feel good again.

stop waiting for bad love to taste sweet.

empathy won't change stones into gold.

time won't change poison into honey.

auspice.

people before the right people find you. let flowers bloom from your losses. some losses are lessons, others are **good omens.**

<u>*eternal.*</u>

she had the kind of energy you only had to feel once to
remember **forever.**

worthy.

i no longer make room for people who won't allow me to make room for myself. i am deserving of space that doesn't come with resentment attached to it when i need it. i am deserving of hiatuses to re-collect myself without it being held against me. i am allowed to **breathe.**

(never let sadness build a permanent place in your heart)

allow sadness to visit. allow sadness a temporary tour. allow
sadness to come by and give you a few lessons, but never allow
sadness to stay. once you've felt everything it's had to say, and once
it's taught you everything you need to know, leave the door open
for **happiness.**

attachments.

attaching titles to connections won't give them more significance.

attaching titles to connections won't prolong their longevity.

attaching titles to connections won't secure them.

attach honesty, transparency, and love to your connections

—that's the energy they require.

i hope,

you never let the fear of being alone

keep you in a space where flowers never grow.

there is nothing romantic about **toxicity.**

within.

when they try to tell you who you are,

you don't have to give ears to their opinion.

you don't have to give a beat to their melody.

you don't have to give a voice to their language.

only you have the power to tell the world who you are.

never.

loyalty should never be the safeguard. you are not obligated to tolerate what isn't good for you just because of how long you've known someone, or because of the things you've experienced together. loyalty should never be the excuse for the lack of **accountability.**

**tranquility.**

there's something about the things left unsaid that

have a way of weighing down on your spirit.

make peace with the pieces that are still heavy on you.

the ones that still linger, the ones that refuse to fade away.

people, the past, experiences. make peace until you feel **lighter.**

<u>*soothing.*</u>

let the version of yourself that you were **teach** you.

let the version of yourself that you are currently **comfort** you.

let the version of yourself that you are becoming **inspire** you.

you are the version that you need and needed to be in every phase of your journey.

to whom this may concern,

don't take my distance personally. i just want us to both bloom within our own spaces, without imposing on each other's growth. our energies will meet again soon.

<u>*fruitless.*</u>

loving someone who feels empty is a unique battle.

it's like pouring water into a cup with holes on the bottom.

no amount of love you show them can convince them

of their wholeness unless they feel whole on their own.

some voids can only be filled by **self.**

<u>art.</u>

re-create yourself, endlessly, shamelessly, recklessly.

re-create yourself, over and over again.

you are never the finished article, and you never have to be.

you are allowed to keep adding color to the

canvas of possibilities that you are until you like what you see.

your intuition has been asking about you. where have you been?

last thing i heard, it called a few times, but you sent it straight
to voicemail. last thing i recall, it sent you a message, and you
left it on read. your heart and mind have sent a search party out
for you because you've been missing lately. you've been listening
to every voice except for the one that speaks to you, you've been
digesting every vibration except for the ones that feed you, you've
been following every path except for the one that leads you back to
yourself. and for what reason? have you let the bad decisions you've
made in the past taint the importance of your internal guide?
have you given up trust in your internal signals because reception
seems low whenever you need it the most? or are you just used to
ignoring internal energy because you've convinced yourself that
your feelings are not important? let go of the reasons, and allow
intuition to be your voice of reason. let the decisions you've made
in the past allow you to grow into the person you need to be, and
let your next decisions be shaped by what is true to you. come back
home, your intuition has been asking about you.

(never compare your healing process with anyone else's. there is a beauty in your process that isn't meant to be replicated or imitated. let it play out the way it should, no matter how hard it seems or how long it takes)

own your healing process; don't shy away from it. it will take a unique shape of its own. allow it to. allow it to be magical, allow it to be bitter, allow it to be relieving, allow it to be sweet. allow it to be beautiful by not comparing your healing process with anyone else's.

and when love isn't enough,

never convince yourself that you aren't enough either. some connections have expiration dates regardless of how hard you try to preserve them. the connections that have died and the connections you couldn't save have nothing to do with your worth.

(knowing your own magic is enough)

if you have to constantly convince them of your **magic,**

they are not deserving of anything you have to offer.

<u>*chapters.*</u>

sometimes, happiness can't find us because we still have a few things to learn from sadness. sometimes, light doesn't appear because we still have a few things to understand about darkness. your low points are not your end points but only **temporary** phases.

<u>incomparable.</u>

she chose happiness, and it was the most **beautiful** fabric i've ever seen on her.

discernment.

i started becoming more intentional about my boundaries when i realized that i was unintentionally inviting unwanted energy into my space. when i made peace with the **realization** that keeping certain people at a distance doesn't make you a bad person when your intentions are good.

(lessons that solitude taught me)

there is a certain intimacy in getting to know yourself that can't be matched. absorb those moments, swim in that solitude, come up for air whenever you need. you can't truly connect with anyone else unless you've connected with yourself **first.**

<u>*ascension.*</u>

you don't have to hold hands and dance with

what you no longer identify with.

you will contradict yourself plenty of times

before you stumble upon your truth

and find what you truly resonate with.

when

was the last time you gave yourself all of you? the last time you gave yourself all of you without saving parts of yourself for other people? when was the last time you were a little selfish with the energy you give out so sparingly? when are you going to change that?

fulfillment.

any connection that requires you to drop your standards to meet the other person at their level is not worth your energy. you are **deserving** of connections that aid in your ascension instead of pulling you underneath the waves.

atonement.

slow down, breathe, **forgive** yourself every chance you can.

don't let one heavy day weigh you down for the rest of your life.

there is much more magic in days ahead.

(be patient. your blessings are on the way)

what you want and where you want to be are taking time,

but don't you see that you are slowly coming into your own?

softly, gently, immaculately. let it happen to you.

don't rush your maturation, your blooming, your process.

everything will happen in the time that it needs to.

she's an ocean;

on some days, floating in her mind is the most calming and peaceful thing you could ever experience, and on other days she's hard to swim in, the waves that she gives off strong, uncontrollable, and intense—but that's the beauty about her. you'll never come across a woman who is so raw, unfiltered, and unapologetic. in a world full of facades and mirages, she remains soaked in her essence. she remains rooted to her truth, no matter how others may feel about her. she remains close to home, even though her vibrations may shake other people's foundations. but she's an ocean; she's not meant to be controlled, she's just meant to be.

(once you understand this, you have made one of the biggest steps in your healing)

old lovers are not enemies.

old lovers are **teachers.**

discovery.

never ignore your fears. there's a reason they exist. find out why.
shine a flashlight on their existence, and ask them questions.
when they started, why they started, how they started. dig into the
truth until you find gold. explore a little deeper until you sense
emancipation.

<u>sincerity.</u>

i can hold you accountable and still love you.

you can hold me accountable and still love me.

this is real energy. this is **real** love.

darling,

you have been taught your whole life that carrying around pain requires strength, but what if i told you that finding the strength to let that pain go is where your true power lies?

and the truth is,

i don't believe that anyone can half-love you. they can take you for granted, but they could never half-love you. because if they truly loved you, they would never be able to halve or quantify what they feel. it's either they love you or they don't.

gentle reminder:

not everything that comes back to you is meant for you.

sometimes things come back as a reminder of just how good you are without them.

(understand this energy)

don't keep me close, keep me **free.**

this will always keep me closer to you than you could ever imagine.

**trust.**

your journey will be misunderstood by many.

at times, your journey won't even make sense to yourself, but trust it nonetheless.

trust the turns and blocks. the stops and dips.

trust that your journey is shaping out the way it's supposed to.

return ticket.

out of all the places i've had the chance to explore, your mind is by far my **favorite.**

transparency.

some people need space to see things clearer. give them that room.

let the distance between the two of you paint the picture they need to see.

sometimes accountability is more **action** than word.

<u>*rare companionship.*</u>

the ones that make silence feel like music,

the ones that make connection feel like oxygen,

the ones that make conversation feel like growth,

keep them around for as long as you can.

darling,

treat yourself a little more softly. your wounds deserve something a little more gentle than salt.

(no one can define how i should feel about myself)

i used to wait for my wholeness to be defined by my connections; now i choose to be whole in spite of them. who is in my life and who decides not to show up do not reflect how full or empty i am. the keys to my wholeness are **firmly** in my grip.

<u>*divine contrasts.*</u>

the most dangerous people are the ones who only stay because there's still much you can do for them. the most valuable people are the ones who stay even when they know that there's not much that you can do.

(healing isn't linear. if you seem to be backpedaling instead of moving forward, there is nothing wrong with that. it will take time to sculpt yourself into the version that you want to be. it will take time to heal from the wounds you are suffering from now or from the ones you've suffered in the past. it will take time to move on from everything that has held you back before, but always remember that steps back are necessary)

understand that steps back are not detrimental to your healing process. take as many steps back as you need, allow yourself to retreat when the waves are too strong, give your path time to clear up during construction—you will find your way **forward** again soon.

shifts of impetus.

someone else's painful narrative is not an excuse for your mistreatment. your soul is not a punching bag. you were not meant to take hits to absorb people's blows just so they can get stronger or just so they can cope. your purpose runs **deeper** than just being someone's safe haven.

to whom this may concern,

all you've known is love that crashes and doesn't flow back to you.
all you've known are lovers who take without the capacity to give.
don't let what's familiar confuse you with what's real—there is
nothing romantic about unrequited love.

darling,

it's exhausting having to explain yourself to people who don't want to understand you. i hope you learn to rest your mind next to ears that have the desire to listen. your concerns hold weight, but only the right ones will know how to carry them.

(i hope you learn to strip yourself of people's expectations of you and learn to exist as the being that you currently are)

it is not your job to manage other people's expectations of you.

that's too much **unnecessary** clothing to wear.

(it's nothing personal; it's just growth)

my growth is too important to hold on to connections that no longer serve me.

my growth is too important to hold on to connections that don't have the desire to be kept.

i will honor the connection i have with **myself** before i honor any connection i may have with anyone else.

(end the narrative that there are good and bad people on your journey. introduce the idea that the people who are put along your path are placed there to help mold you into the masterpiece you need to be going forward)

what if i told you that there are no villains or heroes in your story

but only people and situations placed in your path to help you

bloom into the person you need to be?

soul linguist.

sometimes pain is silent, sometimes it has no words.

sometimes pain is empty, sometimes it can't be filled.

you don't have to find a language for your pain.

you can feel for as long as you need,

until your soul is ready to **speak** again.

(who you are presently is who you need to be right now)

i am constantly outgrowing the person i was yesterday.

the person i'm becoming owes the person i was no **explanation.**

(forgive to feel lighter, but never forget your worth)

if their love ran away at the first sight of struggle,

be wary if their love tries to walk back in when you're at **peace.**

<u>*foresight.*</u>

the goal is to be a little more in love with yourself than you
were yesterday.

i hope

you learn to be everything for yourself before you try to be anything for anyone else. i hope you learn to swim in your own essence before looking for waters elsewhere. i hope you learn that you don't have to rent space in someone else to feel at home.

lantana.

(don't hold on to what needs to leave)

goodbyes can be therapeutic,

allow them to be.

(dear self, i'm sorry)

there are apologies i'm still owed and apologies that will probably never come, but by far the most important apologies are the ones i owe myself. for not thinking i was enough, for not thinking i was **worthy,** for not realizing my magic before.

darling,

you're a rarity. a once-in-a-lifetime kind of love. an experience. you don't have to share yourself with anyone who doesn't realize and treat you as such.

(you are enough)

have you ever wondered about how much of the

pain you carry around actually belongs to you?

have you ever wondered about how much of the

pain you carry around is inherited from lovers, family, and friends?

you can't be medicine to everyone, and that doesn't
make you inadequate.

invaluable.

i have let go of much in the past,

i have compromised many things before,

but my peace of mind is no longer for sale.

i will not give it up for **anything** or **anyone,**

no matter what may be on offer.

familiarity.

too many connections left me alone.

too many connections felt lonely.

too many connections made me forget me,

and that's how i know that the connections

that remind me of who i am are the ones that are meant to **stay.**

lantana.

but you see,

no matter how much love i have for you and no matter how much time i've put into our connection, i could never tolerate mistreatment. i could never stay for what pushes me to leave. the thought of losing you doesn't scare me as much as the thought of losing myself.

oversized.

we've outgrown each other, and that's okay. there's no point in shrinking ourselves to be the people we used to be. memories may exist, but the people we were don't exist anymore. we are who we are right now, and the shoes we used to wear are too small for where we're going. **let go.**

if you're unhappy,

i hope you know that sometimes staying doesn't make you more loyal. if you're unhappy, i hope you know that sometimes staying makes you most disloyal to yourself.

fearless.

i am not afraid of the fire,

i have been burned by lies before.

i am not afraid of the water,

i have drowned in naivety before.

i am not afraid of the wind,

i have lost myself trying to find myself before.

i am not afraid of the earth,

i have been buried by disguised love before.

lantana.

gentle reminder:

spend more time with yourself.

with the parts of you that need more softness.

with the parts of you that feel neglected.

with the parts of you that others found difficult to accept.

massage those parts with **patience,**

feed those parts with **love,**

embrace those parts with open arms.

(what's meant to be will be)

you've made a habit of downplaying your blessings, being unsure of the good things that come your way, being afraid of whether the good things that come will stay, but don't you see that you can never attract what you're not ready for?

lantana.

(open your hands, open your eyes, open your heart)

just because you don't have it now

doesn't mean you'll never get it.

what's yours is already yours.

be **patient** while the universe prepares it for you.

darling,

when you started loving them, you stopped loving yourself, and
with time i hope you realize that there is no worse exchange than
giving up yourself to find a home in someone else.

<u>balance.</u>

you are a symphony.

a consistently beautiful transition of elements.

the relationship you have with yourself will change often.

at times, you will be full of love and at others you will fall out of love with yourself.

be **gentle** with yourself through the transitions.

(some people ignore the work they have to do for themselves and look for you to do it for them. but the truth is healing is an inside job. you can never truly heal unless you are honest with yourself and allow yourself to identify what wounds exist within. you know your wounds better than anyone else. balancing the idea of being there while allowing someone to be there for themselves is challenging but definitely necessary. your peace of mind always comes first)

be careful of the people who always look to you for healing. it is often a sign that there is much healing on their part that they have ignored. out of fear, out of unawareness. be supportive of their healing process, but don't enable their lack of personal accountability.

<u>compartmental.</u>

you could never leave your love halfway with me.

you could never bring your love in parts.

you could never offer me a cup of love and refuse to fill
it to the top.

you see, loving me halfway is just as good as not loving me at all,

and i am much too **full** of love to accept that.

(things she told me)

she told me that her healing began when

she stopped praying for them to come back

and started praying to find herself again.

lessons.

do not mistake having a good time for having chemistry. laughs don't create lovers, and smiles don't create friends. some connections are temporary, and that's all they deserve to be. your intuition will always tell you what you're afraid to tell yourself. **listen** closely.

but you see,

a woman like that is magic. you could never keep her to yourself because she is not yours to keep.

<u>*layers.*</u>

you do not know my pain.

why i use the language i use,

why i love the way i love,

why i color my emotions outside the lines.

you do not know my story.

why i skip certain pages,

why i dwell on others,

why i rush through old chapters.

you have no power over my narrative.

(release, disarm, let go)

you've melted in the arms of lovers who don't know how
to hold you,

and you've been holding yourself **tighter** ever since.

you don't have to let potential love and happiness become victims
of your past.

(the value of your work, ideas, or self is not dictated by anyone but you. no one has the power to take away or add on to the value of everything you are or the value of anything you put into the world. you don't need anyone's approval but your own)

validation is **poison.** your magic doesn't need anyone's approval to be potent.

cease.

the aching never stops until you ask the aching what's wrong.

why it aches when you're alone or why it aches when you're in a crowd.

why it aches by the sun or why it aches when the moon is out.

the aching never stops until you **unpack** all the questions your aching needs to hear.

<u>*sweet delays.*</u>

letting sadness win is not a sign of surrender. sometimes sadness needs to exist for a short while, so you can feel it, so you can understand it, so you can overcome it. sometimes happiness delays its arrival until you've learned everything you need to **learn** from sadness.

truths.

your truth won't sound good to every ear,

your truth won't fit well in every heart,

your truth won't taste sweet on every tongue,

but it's still your truth,

and **no one** can take that away from you.

darling,

i forgive people for choosing to misunderstand me. holding grudges will only weigh me down, and being upset at them won't make them understand me better, and that's something i am learning.

page-turner.

don't try to read me,

i've got chapters in me that you would never understand,

i've got pages in me that you could never make sense of,

i'm a book you could never finish.

(never stop)

you never know who you're inspiring or saving just by being **you.**

(dear self, i hear you)

feeling more and saying less. not as a way of bottling anything in but as a way of validating my own feelings and telling them that i hear them. showing them that i see them. letting them know that they are important and assuring them that they **deserve** to be listened to.

___deep endeavors.___

true love will always try to meet you halfway.

anything else is a facade or a well-disguised lie.

dissimilarities.

the most toxic people love to hold everyone accountable but themselves.

the most poisonous people are quick to shift blame but slow to assume responsibility.

i hope you learn the difference between the ones who need help

and the ones who aren't willing to help themselves.

<u>*recovery.*</u>

your solitude will be too profound for some.

your silence will be too deafening for some.

but how you reclaim your **magic**

and return back home to yourself

are none of their concern.

inward.

i need to make more time for the people i love,

and lately i've been realizing that this means that

i need to start making more time for **me** as well.

lantana.

query:

you want them to give you all of them,

but are you giving yourself all of **you?**

magnifying glass.

and i hope you never get in the habit of planting yourself in spaces that don't support your growth out of fear of being alone. i hope you realize that you don't have to shrink yourself to let others bloom. flowers can grow from solitude, and you are no different.

<u>**nevermore.**</u>

there are untouched lands within me that

have never been explored by lovers who

are too lazy to travel the distance for me,

and i will never allow shallow love to

build a home inside me again.

(soak in how you feel. you are not required to exhibit emotions that
you are not feeling just to make someone else feel comfortable)

happiness can be a heavy thing to carry around,

especially when you're carrying it around for everybody
but **yourself.**

<u>onward.</u>

never let the mistakes you make discredit the growth you've made.

you're allowed to take steps back to move **forward.**

when a passionate woman spills her mind,

you listen with your soul. you hold everything she's pouring out in your hands, leaving no space in between your fingers. you wrap silk around her thoughts and carry them to shore safely. you give her passion air instead of neutralizing it.

(just saying)

do not confuse my unwillingness to interact with you as a sign
of being antisocial.

chances are, your spirit snitched on you and my **intuition**
caught on.

mantra:

i could never be for everyone,

because everyone is not for me.

reinvigorate.

i am releasing myself from more and more every day,

but the thing i have been releasing myself from the most

is the idea that i am not **worthy.** of opportunities, of love, of myself.

see,

i was never placed here to help you increase your self-worth. i was
never placed here to repair parts of you that you felt were broken.
i was never placed here to be your missing link. you loved me,
but you didn't love yourself, and that's why we could never have
worked.

<u>cardio.</u>

i've extended myself to some who were afraid to catch me.

i've extended myself to others who were unwilling to reach me.

i've extended myself to a few who turned the lights off as i got
closer,

but i will no longer stretch my arms out to hold energy that doesn't
want to stay.

(get your head out of the dirt)

the connection ended,

not your narrative.

there is still **life** in your story.

perspective.

i don't want anyone who is afraid to lose me. i'd rather have someone who has faith that i would never leave but still understands that life would go on without me. i'd rather have someone who sees me as an extension of their being instead of the sole reason for their existence.

sadly,

our chapter had to end; but in letting you go i was able to welcome myself back, and there is no greater love story than returning back home to self.

intercession.

i pray you are able to tell the difference between those who accept you for who you are and those who are infatuated by your potential. some are attracted by what you could be, and some are ready to accept you for what you are currently. living up to people's expectations of you is not your duty.

often,

you've been so willing to commit to connections with other people but hesitant to commit to the connection you have with yourself. why do you betray yourself so often to eat meals in other people's hearts when the home within you is missing you at the table?

lantana.

but you see,

one day could never define your worth.

there is too much magic in every inch of you that deserves to
be adored endlessly.

there is too much gold in your bones to only be celebrated for
a few hours.

love kaleidoscopes.

people evolve, and so does their love language. different lovers bring out unique voices within you. different situations change the color of your love. different ideas give your love a second birth. your love language is not required to remain consistent to be **meaningful.**

(find your healing elsewhere)

she feels like freedom,

but she was not placed here to free you.

she might inspire your emancipation,

but she is not responsible for it.

much more.

you are much more divine than you give yourself credit for.

much deeper than the perceptions others have built for you.

you never have to measure your worth by what doesn't come back

and what decides not to stay.

on some days,

i need myself more than i need you, but that doesn't mean that i
love you any less.

i met your mother for the first time today,

and i felt your pain through her eyes. i saw your self-esteem in her body language. i heard your insecurities in her laugh. she gave you life, and in turn, you've given life to the things she dislikes about herself. she experienced life, and in turn, you've adopted her experiences and made them your own. your whole life, you've lived up to skewed ideologies of how a woman should be and how a woman should conduct herself. your whole life, you've looked up to faux versions of what a woman should be and what a woman must consist of to be worthy. your whole life, you've been drinking water from a source dripping in your mother's trauma and heartache, and it's poisoned the perception you have of yourself and the perception you have of the world. you've dived deep to find answers to your mother's pain only to find yourself at her feet every time you come up for air. you've been swimming in your mother's tears for too long, drowning in a battle that was never yours to begin with. there is much she taught you that you must unlearn so you may become your own woman. there is much she taught you that you must unlearn so your daughters may become their own women. there is much she taught you that you must forgive her for so you may finally begin your own healing. i met your mother for the first time today, and i feel like i finally met you.

i met your father for the first time today,

and i spotted his facade from miles away. i grasped his essence from his mannerisms, and i recognized his energy in you. he masked his insecurities with fake steel, and he carried his poorly hidden wounds in his back pocket. his masculinity was playing an intense tug-of-war with his softness, and his feminine energy was playing a game of hide-and-seek with his ego. but still, he carried himself around with the same assertiveness of his forefathers—not by choice but because of habit, because of training, and because of fear. but you still love him. i mean, why wouldn't you? this is the man who held your hand in the rain when the world tried to drown you. this is the man who protected you from the weight of the world when it threatened to crush you. this is the man who sacrificed parts of himself to ensure that you went to sleep not having to fear the world. but parts of you resent him. parts of you resent him because he carries around unhealed trauma that he has yet to resolve, and it's put a damper on your connection at times. parts of you resent him because every morning you wake up and look in the mirror and you're reminded of just how much you look like him. parts of you resent him because he spent too much time trying to protect you instead of spending time trying to understand you. as you get to know yourself further in life, and as you peel your internal layers one by one, continue to forgive him, continue to pray for him, continue to love him, because you deserve to feel light, and resentment can be heavy. i met your father for the first time today, and i feel like i finally met you.

unashamed.

my love can be messy.

i over pour sometimes and it spills over.

i add too much sugar to the pot and it gets sticky.

i bake it in my heart for too long and it burns fingers.

but i will never apologize for it. not for the intensity of it,

not for the quality of it, not for **nothing.**

(spend more time with you)

some connections crumble, not because we don't want to learn their
love language

but simply because we haven't learned our **own.**

sometimes.

i think of you sometimes,

but not in the same way.

not in the way you would desire and hope.

not in a way of reliving and reminiscing.

not in a romantic or longing sense

but more in a sense of relief and gratitude.

you were the lesson i needed to get to where i am today.

<u>*distance.*</u>

you've been chasing so many things intensely that you've unknowingly been running further away from **yourself.**

return to sender.

i left you where you left me, but you will never find me where we last left. my growth would never allow me to occupy old spaces for comfort. my growth would never allow me to revisit what i left behind, because there is much more ahead of me.

dry waterfalls.

there are tears you haven't given the space to flow because you feel like your pain isn't important enough to be understood. there are tears you haven't given the space to flow because you've lived believing that strength lies in your emotional fortitude.

heal those spaces.

notes on overdue apologies:

there are many people who you are going to have to learn to forgive even with an absence of an apology. not because you don't deserve one but only because you deserve peace of mind.

we often attach the importance of forgiveness to words when the truth is not everyone will be willing to or can truly comprehend the language of your pain.

waiting for an apology that is never coming will only poison you slowly. waiting for an apology that is never coming will only give you a false sense of your worth. waiting for an apology that is never coming will only steal your peace and replace it with grief.

(it's okay to be, without trying too hard being)

stillness is something i am practicing.

understanding that sometimes there is growth in doing nothing.

releasing myself from the idea that i need to be in command of
every situation.

i **refuse** to give uncontrollable situations and desires power over my
actions and narrative.

justified.

you've made magic out of your wounds and that gives you every right to be cautious about who is allowed to experience you. the fruits of your healing are not for **everyone** to bite into.

darling,

many will be intimidated by your narrative. many will take issue with it because they don't want to be left behind, and others will be indifferent to your narrative because they are not aligned with their own. you don't have to put full stops in your story for anyone.

**opportunities.**

it's unfair. they lit a fire in your soul but disappeared shortly after. you deserve more, but this is the chance you've always needed to learn to light your own fires and keep yourself warm instead of waiting for someone else.

<u>*boundaries.*</u>

there are walls that exist within me that i

must break down for my own growth,

but there are also walls that exist within me

that i must keep up so people know that

i am not available at their convenience.

(you are free to keep your energy to yourself)

your solitude isn't a sin. you don't have to drown in waves that feel unfamiliar just because it's what other people are comfortable with. you don't have to suffocate your being just because it's what gives other people life. soak in your energy with **no guilt.**

lantana.

awareness.

it took me losing everything that i thought was meant to stay

for me to realize that i was always **enough** for me.

(goodbye and good riddance)

i used to justify people's departures by finding faults in myself and creating false narratives about me that validate their inability to stay. now when they leave, i open the door for them and stick the list of excuses i could've attached to them in the bag they're leaving with.

<u>*when?*</u>

when did you start apologizing for your love tasting too sweet?

when did you start apologizing for your love feeling too warm?

when did you start apologizing for your love being too loud?

when did you become an apology instead of just **being** love?

invisible locks.

there are parts of you that are scared of leaving your comfort zone because you are afraid that you might fail and have nothing to fall back on if you do. **leave** the false safety net that you've been conditioned into—your comfort zone doesn't deserve power over your narrative.

lantana.

<u>priorities.</u>

the focus has been myself

and will continue to be myself.

plucking at my petals and

shaking my roots

will not halt my growth.

self-sabotage.

you've dressed your trauma in denial for lovers who romanticize perfection in fear that they might leave if they see the real you, while ignoring everything that exists underneath your layers of pain, but i hope you know that unaddressed trauma breeds the most toxic connections.

lantana.

(not what you wanted to hear but what you needed to)

i never gave up on you.

i only gave me more of a chance.

home sweet home.

i told her to go where she was celebrated, and she went straight back to **herself.**

<u>*synergy.*</u>

the **more** energy you give to the things you've lost,

the **less** room you make for beautiful things to enter your life.

watch.

water your bad days with love and patience,

watch as **flowers** grow from it tomorrow.

transition.

you will grow from everything you encounter.

you will grow from everyone you encounter.

you will grow from everywhere you encounter.

you will grow.

Andrews McMeel Publishing
a division of Andrews McMeel Universal
1130 Walnut Street, Kansas City, Missouri 64106

www.andrewsmcmeel.com

23 24 25 26 27 RLP 14 13 12 11 10

ISBN: 978-1-5248-6041-7

Library of Congress Control Number: 2020934324

Editor: Patty Rice
Art Director/Designer: Tiffany Meairs
Production Editor: Elizabeth A. Garcia
Production Manager: Carol Coe

ATTENTION: SCHOOLS AND BUSINESSES
Andrews McMeel books are available at quantity discounts with
bulk purchase for educational, business, or sales promotional use.
For information, please e-mail the Andrews McMeel Publishing
Special Sales Department: sales@amuniversal.com.

Enjoy *Flowers on the Moon* as an audiobook, wherever audiobooks are sold.